What Our Readers Have Said...

"Although I consider myself a seasoned sales professional, it is helpful to have past learning's refreshed. The books were also beneficial because of the information concerning 'trends' in the sales relationship. The sales process should be viewed as dynamic since business relationships change regularly."

•

"For the particular business I am in and the type of sales calls I have, I find that the books in the Pinpoint Sales Training Series are very often applicable to how I conduct business. I would recommend them to other sales people, just not ones that are in my industry."

•

"These books provide very good concepts. It fits in well with the Bell Leadership training program that I attended in November."

•

"I use this material in these books and apply it to my customers and other employees I work with."

•

"I would like to know other topics. Is there anything on Production Management or Consultative Selling or Time Management?"

•

"These books are great tools that should be used as guidelines for our everyday

supervisory practices. You need to take the time to do a short self-evaluation when reading them."

•

"The Pinpoint Training Series delivers information that could be used in a lot different areas."

•

"I like this because I can take them with me to read at a convenient time. I feel the little time I have to spend in the office is best use on activities that directly relate to revenue opportunities. I like the short amount of time it takes to keep up with these."

•

"I prefer the self-study approach; it fits in with my schedule."

•

"My thought is that the real value of these books comes into effect when doing the action plans."

•

"Short and sweet. These books are easy to comprehend."

•

"I have enjoyed reading these books. They are relevant to today's work environment and the ongoing change in the way we manage our workforce."

•

"I do feel that these books have been very helpful to me at my job."

•

"I think a lot of the recommendations in these books are very useful, and can be applicable to everyday situations. If nothing else, it's a good reference guide to fall back upon if a situation arises in the future."

•

"These books are relevant to today's work environment and the ongoing change in the way we manage our workforce."

•

Consultative Sales Strategies

Pinpoint Sales Skill Development Training Series

TIMOTHY F. BEDNARZ

MAJORIUM
BUSINESS PRESS

Pinpoint Sales Skill Development Training Series
"Consultative Sales Strategies"
Timothy F. Bednarz

Graphic design: Monika Pawlak

Majorium Business Press
2025 Main Street
Stevens Point, WI 54481
715.342.1018 • 800.654.4935

ISBN 978-1-882181-88-9

Printed in the United States of America

Introduction

The Pinpoint Sales Skill Development Training Series is designed for targeted training and education regarding increased improvement in a specific skill or competency.

Each book within this series is designed to be easy to use, understand and apply to your job. It can be used as a basis for training individuals, as a discussion guide or as a personal training tool.

Each chapter within this book discusses a specific concept. When you have completed all eight chapters you should have a 360° perspective of the topic.

Additionally, each chapter is divided into specific sections:

- The first section provides you with an overview of the topic
- The Implications section discusses why the concept is important, and why it is important to learn and apply.
- The Strategies, Tips & Techniques to Apply section teaches how to use and apply the particular concept to your work.
- The Points to Ponder section gives you something to think about or to be discussed with a group setting. These are questions not meant to be immediately answered, but to be pondered over time.
- The Training Activity section provides you with the tools to transfer what you have learned to your job. It is designed to help create an action plan to effectively apply the concept.

Each of the topics in this series is time-tested and proven in the marketplace. They have been used by thousands of employees as training tools. Many of the users have commented that what made these books valuable, was the ability to refer to them when a problem surfaced. They indicated that they remembered reading about the exact problem. They referred back to these books and found an appropriate solution.

You will find them equally valuable as a resource in your professional development library.

Table of Contents

LEARNING OBJECTIVES:

- The concept and elements of consultative selling.
- To identify why consultative selling skills can be beneficial.
- To avoid the problems and pitfalls associated with consultative selling.
- To apply effective consultative selling techniques.
- To evaluate consultative selling strategies.

1

Why Consultative Selling Is Important

Salespeople must utilize their expertise and experience as a sustainable benefit to the customer and as a means of competitively positioning themselves. They require relational skills that allow them to build and sustain long-term relationships with their prospects and customers. In this manner, they develop the levels of rapport required to sustain the relationship so that it resists competitive pressures as well as economic cycles and downturns.

IMPLICATIONS – WHAT THIS MEANS TO YOU

The purpose of consultative selling is to enhance the customer relationship with the salesperson. This is in contrast to the typical sales goal of selling a product or service without regard to the development of a relationship. Consultative selling techniques allow salespeople to leverage their experience, expertise and network of contacts to develop relationships. The motivation is one of service rather than sales. As relationships evolve and develop, prospects and customers learn to trust the salesperson as a friend and adviser. When salespeople are able to elevate themselves to this position, the recommendations they make concerning their products and services are not as threatening as the salesperson motivated only to sell a product and service. When a sales recommendation is made, initial sales resistance is lowered considerably.

Consultative selling methods allow salespeople to use their experience and expertise to gain a competitive advantage. Within today's selling environment, these techniques offer unique advantages that most competitors will find difficult to match.

STRATEGIES, TIPS & TECHNIQUES TO APPLY

When salespeople employ consultative selling techniques they must keep in mind not only their own interests and the interests of their company, but also those of their customers. The relationship between sales and service becomes critical in the consultative selling environment. Because of this, salespeople must be aware at all times of the ways that they approach their customers.

The Customer's Needs

Rather than sell customers on various products and services, salespeople actually are serving their needs by introducing them to potentially new products and services that might address current problems and issues. Salespeople are also identifying needs that the customer may not be aware of.

Sounding Board

As salespeople perfect consultative selling techniques and use them to mold relationships, they begin to serve as the sounding board for customer problems. In this manner, salespeople can both empathize with the customer and suggest solutions to their problems. While obvious solutions may include the products or services salespeople have to offer, in many cases their recommendations are unrelated to their own products and services. In this regard, they are acting as a true consultant to both their customers and prospects, which strengthens trust, rapport, and the relationship. When it comes time to make actual product or service recommendations, customers are more likely to listen to and trust what salespeople have to say and offer.

Problem Solver

As salespeople develop into customer sounding boards and establish trust and rapport, certain information may be shared with them. They are being trusted with problems, concerns and issues that prospects and customers are dealing with. This places salespeople in unique positions as problem solvers. While their products and services do not always answer the problems and issues that customers and prospects have, their expertise, experience and network of contacts allow them to offer other types of assistance. They are able to bring their available resources to bear to produce a solution that helps their prospects or customers. This enhances their credibility and elevates them as a trusted adviser to their prospects and customers.

Trouble Shooter

In a unique position as a liaison between their company and their customers, salespeople are able to recommend products and services that meet the customer's needs and requirements. Salespeople become valuable conduits of information, expertise and knowledge between their company and customers, thus providing a valuable resource to both the company and customer.

Expediter

Consultative selling requires salespeople to expand their abilities beyond the realm of selling a product or service to their customers. Salespeople who employ these techniques will ensure that all elements of the sale are expedited and that customer satisfaction is assured by prompt delivery, installation and consumer education. This emphasizes their service while enhancing levels of trust and credibility.

Matchmaker

As salespeople mesh the needs of the customer with the needs of their company, they effectively become matchmakers: they identify for their company the best possible customer opportunities while matching the best product and service recommendations for their customers. When using consultative selling techniques, the needs of one party do not outweigh the needs of another. Consequently, salespeople create a win-win situation for both their company and customers.

Negotiator

Within most sales environments, each party seeks the best deal for themselves. Salespeople are motivated to get the highest commission, their companies are motivated to get the highest sale, and the customer is motivated to get the best price. When salespeople use effective consultative selling techniques, they balance the needs of all three parties. No one party is favored over the needs of the others. All needs are balanced and met creating a win-win situation for all involved.

POINTS TO PONDER — SOMETHING TO THINK ABOUT

1. Where do you place your emphasis: on selling your customers or servicing them?
2. How do you typically build trust and rapport with your customers?

TRAINING ACTIVITY — APPLICATION & ACTION PLAN

On a sheet of paper define all elements of a typical customer relationship, from the initiation of the sales process, through the sale and including all aspects of service and relationship building.

1. Diagram all of these key points and label each element as to whether it sells the customer or services them.
2. Identify additional elements that you can include in your customer relationship that helps you be of better service to the customer.
3. Determine how you can implement these elements.

2

Factors to Consider When Applying Consultative Selling Techniques

Effective consultative selling techniques allow salespeople to bring all critical areas of sales knowledge and expertise to bear on a customer contact. Equipped with this knowledge, salespeople are able to build relationships and enhance rapport with their customers.

IMPLICATIONS – WHAT THIS MEANS TO YOU

Technology and increased global competition have made customers more knowledgeable, sophisticated and demanding. Also dealing with more complex problems and issues, customers are seeking more knowledge and expertise to assist them in the management of their business. As such, salespeople are faced with increased demands to produce more results more quickly. They must earn the right to do business with prospects and customers, and that right is earned through the application of their expertise and experience.

Consultative selling techniques provide salespeople with the tools they need to successfully package their expertise and experience in a way that adds value for the customer. As companies seek customized solutions, products and services, salespeople need the expertise to be able to address and meet their needs. The factors salespeople must consider when employing consultative selling techniques provide them with the expertise and knowledge to successfully address these customer needs and issues.

STRATEGIES, TIPS & TECHNIQUES TO APPLY

Effective consultative selling techniques are based on three of the four pillars of successful selling: customer, product and company knowledge. The fourth pillar is competitive knowledge. In order to successfully apply consultative selling, salespeople must blend their in-depth knowledge and expertise in each of these three critical areas into a polished and effective approach.

Many salespeople fail to acquire sufficient knowledge in each of the three critical areas. Without this knowledge, salespeople are unable to create the detailed analysis that allows them to blend their experience and expertise and to craft a unique solution for their customers. In many cases, salespeople have only superficial knowledge of the products they sell, the company they represent and the customers they serve. They only develop sufficient knowledge to, in their opinion, "get the job done." They fail to understand how in-depth knowledge, linked with experience and expertise, provides them with the tools to craft strong and competitive solutions.

Consultative selling requires that salespeople creatively think about all three areas. Without this knowledge, they are only offering a shallow solution to problems that are often complex. This is why salespeople often fail to land sales. An examination of these three areas should highlight the difference between superficial and in-depth knowledge.

Product Knowledge

Most salespeople have a fairly large catalog of products and services. Typically salespeople will select three or four major products they feel they can move. In this capacity, salespeople will typically focus on the features and benefits that those three or four major products offer. However, in-depth knowledge must go beyond those features and benefits to include customers' perspectives or viewpoints of what those products or services will do for them. It includes understanding both the tangible and intangible benefits of each product and service and establishing a quantitative value for each.

Product knowledge should also include a balanced knowledge of the full spectrum of what the company has to offer in terms of products and services. Salespeople should not fall into the trap of identifying only three or four major products they wish to sell, but understand how the full breadth and scope of products and services will be of more value to their prospects and customers.

Customer Knowledge

In many salespeople's minds, customer knowledge is defined as a customer profile. This includes the basic information needed to identify the customer—company name, buyer, decision maker, current products and services, and applications. Salespeople might also include other information they acquired through numerous calls and visits, including wants, needs, problems, issues and other concerns. However, this is often where customer knowledge ends.

Very few salespeople take the time to understand the customer's motivation for buying a product or service. They fail to take into account the customers' perspectives or viewpoints, including how customers perceive a product or service in relation to its value and price.

Company Knowledge

It is surprising how little knowledge many salespeople have of their company. Many are ignorant of its capacities and capabilities, terms, conditions and additional aspects that impact customers. Until salespeople understand what their company is capable of delivering in terms of services, values and other critical aspects of the sale, they are incapable of leveraging this information to their advantage. They are unable to blend this knowledge with their product and customer knowledge to offer a credible solution. This information is as essential to the success of the sale as customer and product information.

POINTS TO PONDER — SOMETHING TO THINK ABOUT

1. What is the breadth and scope of your customer, product and company knowledge?
2. How successfully are you able to leverage your experience and expertise in providing value to your prospects and customers?

TRAINING ACTIVITY — APPLICATION & ACTION PLAN

Create a consultative protocol for each of your major products and services.

1. Define the features, advantages and benefits of each major product.
2. Create a product profile sheet for each product based on this information. Develop sheets that can be used as customer handouts during your sales calls and for follow-ups.

3

How Consultative Selling Affects Sales

If salespeople wish to succeed in an increasingly competitive sales environment, it is necessary to employ more sophisticated selling skills that begin to match how prospects and customers purchase products, goods and services. This includes understanding the motivation of prospects and customers and the effect of matching goods and services with wants and needs. This is often more work than many salespeople are willing to devote. However, the impact and effect of more sophisticated sales techniques, such as consultative selling, are highly effective and productive, especially in the long term.

IMPLICATIONS – WHAT THIS MEANS TO YOU

Most salespeople are looking for ways to create a competitive edge for themselves. It is increasingly difficult for salespeople to differentiate themselves and have their message clearly heard by prospects and customers. At the same time, prospects and customers are starving for expertise and knowledge. They actively seek and welcome sources that can provide them solutions to pressing problems and concerns and actively seek out individuals who can help them become more effective, efficient and productive in their business.

This is important for salespeople to understand because the use of consultative selling techniques allows them to elevate themselves above the competitive din of other salespeople's products and services. It allows them to leverage their strengths, knowledge and expertise into a competitive advantage that is welcomed by customers and prospects as they seek ways to improve their own business practices. The time and effort salespeople invest in learning and applying these techniques will pay off in the long term. It should be noted these techniques take time to produce results. However, once successfully implemented and accepted by prospects and customers, salespeople will find them very profitable.

STRATEGIES, TIPS & TECHNIQUES TO APPLY

Consultative selling does take more time and effort. Some salespeople will argue that the time and effort is better spent on direct contact with customers. However, consultative selling techniques do have distinct advantages and benefits that other forms of selling do not offer.

Increased Trust and Rapport

Trust and rapport, as most salespeople know, are requirements for any sales relationship. The effective application of consultative selling over extended periods of time increases levels of trust and rapport experienced by salespeople.

The element of trust is not something that can be immediately achieved, as prospects and customers are leery of many salespeople and their personal motives. Over time, the application of consultative selling techniques reduces the skepticism of many prospects and customers. Not all customers and prospects will immediately develop high levels of trust and rapport. However, salespeople should experience elevated levels of trust and rapport across their entire customer base as they practice these techniques.

Elevate Salesperson as Adviser

It is impractical for salespeople to expect customers and prospects to embrace them immediately as a consultant and adviser. This takes time and is developed as the relationship with the customer grows. If prospects and customers observe that specific salespeople are not solely motivated to make the sale, and are there to help expand and build their business, then they will be slowly elevated to the status of trusted advisers. Salespeople will need to invest themselves in this process by sharing their expertise and experience in a manner that does not immediately result in a sale. In doing so prospects and customers will ultimately trust them and learn to rely on them to help develop credible solutions.

Reduces Resistance

Over extended periods of time, once trust and rapport are established and salespeople are regarded as trusted advisers, they will experience reduced sales resistance. Prospects and customers will no longer question their motivation to be of service to them. They understand salespeople are in the business of selling their products and services, but also see that the salesperson desires to be of service. Therefore, when a product or service is recommended, customers and prospects become more amenable and open to recommendations.

Customizes Solutions

The application of consultative selling techniques allows salespeople to employ their knowledge and expertise and the available advantages and benefits offered by their company's products and services to create customized solutions that meet a specific customer's needs. The forces of change and technology indicate that this trend will become stronger all the time.

Help Customers Buy

When salespeople employ consultative selling techniques, they embed themselves into their customer's business. In this capacity, they are able to educate rather than sell customers and prospects by helping them buy products and services that meet their specific needs. Prospects and customers perceive the change in salespeople's motivation from sales to helping them buy.

Differentiates and Positions Salespeople

Salespeople will not feel the impact of the application of consultative selling techniques immediately. It takes time to develop the trust and rapport required for this technique to take hold. However, once salespeople successfully employ and implement this approach and it is recognized, they will find that it clearly differentiates and positions them against the competition.

In this manner, salespeople are more openly received by prospects and customers, especially in a time when many refuse to answer phone calls, voicemails and email. Consultative selling techniques allow salespeople, once they have developed a reputation for their expertise, to be more welcomed. They will find that their calls and emails are addressed and answered more promptly, especially when prospects and customers understand that the message is not to sell, but to be helpful and of assistance.

POINTS TO PONDER — SOMETHING TO THINK ABOUT

1. In what ways have you been able to effectively reduce overall sales resistance?
2. How have you been able to communicate your message through the competitive din that many prospects and customers are surrounded with?

TRAINING ACTIVITY — APPLICATION & ACTION PLAN

Identify ways that you can elevate yourself into a consultative role with your prospects and customers.

1. Determine the type of information, expertise and knowledge that your customers and prospects are seeking to help them build a more productive business.
2. Identify the areas of expertise and knowledge that you can specifically offer to your prospects and customers.
3. Determine the match between the customer's needs and what you have to offer.
4. Identify additional areas in which you can develop experience and expertise in order to add value for your prospects and customers.

4

Common Problems and Pitfalls in Consultative Selling

The logic of consultative selling, also known as value-added or application selling, produces results because it advocates the concept of the salesperson as consultant, approaching new customers and prospects and solving complex business problems for them. As with any effective sales technique, salespeople should be aware that there are pitfalls and problems that need to be identified and avoided.

IMPLICATIONS — WHAT THIS MEANS TO YOU

Over the past several decades there has been a fundamental shift in the way companies do business. The advancement of technology has enabled them to quickly create higher quality products. The downside is that many products are similar to the competition's. Additionally, many companies have been making inroads to drive down costs—a trend that has accelerated over the years due to the recession experienced by most companies. The result is many companies are focusing on the bottom-line price rather than the value received from the goods and services they purchase.

Consultative selling techniques stress value over price by using the salesperson's expertise and knowledge to craft unique solutions for their prospects and customers. Many may question the validity of this technique when trends demonstrate that companies are focusing on price over value. Obviously, this impacts the salesperson's ability to generate sales.

Consultative selling, while it has its pitfalls and problems, is still considered a valid and effective sales approach. It still focuses on customers and their needs and seeks to develop solid relationships with them. Salespeople need to consider how to balance the consultative selling approach so that they do not provide too much expertise and knowledge prior to the sale. They should understand how to incorporate their value-added service into the sale. Otherwise, many will find their expertise and knowledge used against them and to their competitor's benefit.

STRATEGIES, TIPS & TECHNIQUES TO APPLY

The concept of consultative selling dictates that salespeople become intimately acquainted with their products and use their extensive knowledge and expertise of product advantages and processes to rework and save customers both time and money. While this is a desirable and effective approach, there are a number of pitfalls and problems that salespeople should be aware of.

Mature Product

As products and industries mature, the salesperson's ability to consult on product advantages greatly diminishes. This is because mature products offer fewer applications that deliver technical advantages for the manufacturer and its distributors.

Additionally, due to technological advancements, the majority of products being sold within any major market are essentially the same. The product space between these products has shrunk with little or no way to differentiate one from another. Consequently, in many sectors, major sales hinge on minor differences. From the customer's perspective, when there is little or nothing to differentiate one product from another, the clear deciding factor becomes price.

Consultative selling is an attempt to minimize these disadvantages by leveraging salespeople's experience and expertise to their advantage. In many instances, it is these factors that determine the final sale.

Price

During recessionary times there is increased pressure on buyers to shop for the best price. Salespeople are not guaranteed to win the sale because they have offered the best proposal to reduce overall costs. This bottom-line thinking is in direct contrast to the buying patterns of the 1990s.

More companies are considering price as the determining factor as long as products and services meet their basic specifications and perform the job adequately. While value has always been a strong sales component, in many instances buyers have no choice but to base their decision on price.

Leveraging Expertise

The one action that infuriates salespeople above all others is when prospects and customers take their work delivered in a proposal and give it to the competition to bid against.

In these cases, salespeople consulted with their prospects and customers and analyzed their business to make recommendations. In many instances, salespeople have uncovered hidden needs and problems, developed viable solutions and made strong product recommendations. They have invested considerable time and effort to help prospects and customers improve their business. Unfortunately, in certain cases, customers will use their work as the basis of new product specifications. Rather than keeping information confidential and proprietary, they openly share it with the competition, the end result being that the sale is delivered to the lowest bidder, who has benefited from the salesperson's diligent contribution.

In most cases this infuriates salespeople who feel that the prospect or customer has acted unethically. Rather than imbedding themselves in the prospect or customer's business, their actions have actually made them more vulnerable to the competition.

Free Service

The consultative selling approach often subsidizes the competition due to the fact that time and effort is invested in analyzing the customer's business and advising them of best practices to improve their efficiency and productivity.

The obvious solution is for salespeople to charge for this service, as it offers a distinct value to the customer. However, this is difficult, if not impossible; customers are not apt to pay for a service they can get free elsewhere. Additionally, prospects and customers think of the service being provided by salespeople as more or less free, since there are no visible costs associated with the service. This places salespeople in a dilemma of either providing a valuable service or withholding services altogether. In either case, it results in a diminished competitive advantage, and can undermine their credibility.

POINTS TO PONDER — SOMETHING TO THINK ABOUT

1. Have you experienced a situation where you have invested time and effort to assist your prospect and customer only to lose the order to the lowest priced competitor that has used your recommendations as the basis of their proposition?
2. Are you finding it increasingly difficult to differentiate your products and services as prospects and customers seek lower and lower prices?

TRAINING ACTIVITY — APPLICATION & ACTION PLAN

On a sheet of paper, create two columns titled, "Before the Sale" and "After the Sale."

1. Make a list of the available services you can provide to your prospects or customers to assist them to become more effective, efficient and productive by using your products and services.
2. Identify the services you feel are essential for the sale to be made. Indicate this next to each one.

3. Determine the services that you can offer after the sale, and as a condition of the sale.
4. Redefine the package of services that you can utilize in a consultative selling environment without undermining your position and diminishing your expertise.

5

Consultative Selling Techniques

Salespeople employing consultative selling techniques bring with them a "toolbox" of time- and market-tested solutions stemming from other successful customer applications. These include solutions their company has developed in the past, such as cost-effective measures and production shortcuts. Most importantly, these salespeople bring the experience gained from past successes to bear in solving a customer's current problems.

IMPLICATIONS — WHAT THIS MEANS TO YOU

In the past, salespeople were the primary providers of information concerning the products and services they sold. However, increased availability of information, primarily through the Internet, has shifted the salesperson's primary role. The use and existence of salespeople has to be reexamined in light of market changes in customer behaviors. While the traditional role of providing transactional sales is still valid, the need to add value to the buying process becomes increasingly important.

Many prospects and customers are relatively sophisticated and have ready access to information over the Internet. They do not require salespeople to make a buying decision. In many instances, transactional sales are taking place electronically, without the presence of a salesperson. However, for complex, customized products and services, salespeople are needed to add value. While there are problems and pitfalls associated with this approach, it is a growing role for salespeople.

The rising costs of making a physical sales call dictate that salespeople who use in-person contacts as their primary selling method must maximize their impact and insure that value is added during the sales process to justify the high cost of the call. Consequently, effective selling techniques must be employed to maximize the value of each sales call.

STRATEGIES, TIPS & TECHNIQUES TO APPLY

Consultative selling is based upon the need-satisfaction buying theory. This approach is a customer-centric sales process based upon the identification of the customer's needs and salespeople's ability to solve them through the application of their products and services. The process is also value-added: salespeople add value to their products or services by offering recommendations or solutions to help customers become more productive. This method leads customers through the following steps to make a buying decision, especially when it concerns complex and expensive products and services.

Needs Identification

No sale will be made until prospects and customers know that a problem exists and understand the seriousness and extent of it. The role of the salesperson is to help customers and prospects recognize and define the problems and needs that impact their business. Salespeople should use various probing and questioning techniques to uncover obvious and hidden problems and concerns. Even if prospects and customers are aware of these problems and concerns, salespeople can add value by helping them recognize and define problems and needs in a new and different way.

Evaluation of Options

One major pitfall that many salespeople fall into is assuming that customers and prospects know as much about their products and services as they do. They assume their audience possesses the same level of knowledge and expertise and does not need to be educated in the specific nuances of their products and services.

Consultative salespeople understand the value of educating their prospects and customers about their products and clearly demonstrate that they offer the best available option. They understand that there are superior solutions, options and approaches that prospects and customers may not have understood, considered or even been aware of.

Helping the Customer Buy

Consultative selling focuses on educating customers and helping them make the best possible choice to meet their specific needs and resolve problems. As a consultant, salespeople place themselves in a position of helping customers and prospects evaluate and analyze the available alternatives. In this capacity, salespeople evaluate and analyze various options for their customers while influencing them to make a purchase based upon their recommendations. Helping customers overcome and remove any possible obstacles to the acquisition of products and services creates value. This includes handling questions and objections, as well as finalizing details required to conclude the sale.

Commitment

The flow of the consultative selling process leads prospects and customers to a logical conclusion: a commitment to buy. Salespeople arrive at this point by studying customers' businesses, educating them about the best options available and, influencing them during the evaluation and analysis stage. Once they arrive at this point, salespeople add value by making it easy for them to purchase. Since the entire selling process is customer-centric, the actual purchase should be the same. It should be user-friendly, painless, convenient and hassle-free. Salespeople should be facilitators who smooth out any bumps and ensure customers do not become reluctant due to transactional problems.

Implementation

Transactional salespeople typically disappear once the sale has been made. One of the fundamental keys of consultative selling is developing trust and rapport. If salespeople hope to retain credibility, they must add value by remaining visible once the sale has been made. They should remain active in the implementation phase. This means facilitating the delivery and installation of products or services, and training and educating end users concerning the best practices of how that product or service should be used.

Salespeople educated in customer-focused selling, application selling, value-added selling and other customer-centric methods will see similarities in all of these sales methods. Additionally, they will note consultative selling is a blending of effective sales tools and techniques that most salespeople are acquainted with. It is the blending and application of these methods that make them effective.

POINTS TO PONDER — SOMETHING TO THINK ABOUT

1. What results have you achieved using consultative selling or a similar sales approach?
2. Do you feel these sales techniques address the biggest problems and concerns that you are experiencing with your prospects and customers?

TRAINING ACTIVITY — APPLICATION & ACTION PLAN

Listed below are five primary sales methods:

- Transactional Sales
- Value-added Sales
- Application Sales
- Consultative Sales
- Customer-focused Sales

1. Identify two or three of the primary selling applications you are familiar with.

2. Compare and contrast these selling applications with each other.
3. Identify the similarities and differences.
4. Determine the strengths and weaknesses of each.

6

Additional Consultative Selling Techniques

Consultative selling initially establishes a relationship that is maintained throughout and developed to create enthusiastic customers, who ultimately become advocates for a company and its products and services.

IMPLICATIONS – WHAT THIS MEANS TO YOU

Salespeople should be aware that consultative selling techniques—as well as any other customer-centric sales processes—and the actual sale are only the beginning of the customer relationship. While consultative selling is designed to allow salespeople to effectively build relationships and generate sales, it is not designed to create the one-time sale that transactional sales techniques often generate. Rather, it is designed to create a relationship that enhances satisfaction and generates a long-term customer that ultimately becomes part of the salesperson's book of business. Additionally, salespeople are creating a number of customer advocates, who ultimately enhance their ability to generate leads.

This is important for salespeople to understand because when customers become advocates, they become open and active voices for the salesperson, his or her company, and its products and services. They generate word-of-mouth advertising. At the same time, they generate networks of prospects referred directly to the salesperson. This is the most desirable position for salespeople to be in. The time and effort invested in customers who permanently become advocates will generate additional sales identified not by salespeople, but by the happy customers.

STRATEGIES, TIPS & TECHNIQUES TO APPLY

The goals of consultative selling are accomplished by adding value with the needs satisfaction buying process. A deeper examination of this process and the consultative selling message includes the following:

Needs Discovery

The most important value-added activity salespeople can perform is discovering and understanding the customer's needs. Without knowing their needs, the salesperson cannot possibly recommend any products or services that will address and solve the customer's needs or problems. There are three primary dimensions of needs discovery:

Asking Questions – Questions are one of the most effective ways to involve the potential customer in the sales process. The use of appropriate questions reduces tension and builds trust because they communicate interests in the customer's needs. Without the use of questions, salespeople effectively close the door on two-way communication.

Listening and Acknowledgement – Most individuals fail to hear approximately 75% of what is spoken to them by other people. This ratio is improved by developing active listening skills that takes into consideration both the verbal and nonverbal signals transmitted by prospects and customers. Additionally, active listening involves three specific techniques:

- Soliciting feedback
- Taking notes
- Paraphrasing

Establishing Buying Motive – Buyers will usually have either a rational or emotional reason for making a purchase. While prospects and customers may state many needs, there usually is a primary motive for making a purchase.

Demonstration

Tangible demonstrations that reveal how products and services work and accomplish things is one way to show how they can effectively meet the customer's needs.

Overcoming Buyer Resistance

In many sales situations, overcoming resistance means handling objections, connoting a win-lose type of negotiation. Rather, salespeople should use a two-way problem solving dialogue and negotiate in an atmosphere of trust.

Buyer resistance is minimized by:

- Clarifying facts
- Acknowledging partial validity of objections, but offsetting it with superior benefits
- A trial offer to reduce the customer's perceived risks
- The use of superior benefits to outweigh the competitor's offering
- Third-party endorsements
- Restating the benefits and suggesting an obvious choice
- Using a demonstration as tangible supporting proof

Closing and Confirming the Sale

The closing of the sale asks for the order whereas confirming the sale reassures the buyer that they have made the right choice. It is easier to close the sale if the consultative selling process has been closely followed and properly handled. It is part of the logical conclusion or outcome of a successful selling process.

Closings can be facilitated by:

- Focusing on the dominant buying motives
- Negotiating the tough points before attempting to close
- Avoiding surprises at the close
- Not isolating the prospect or customer during the sale
- Displaying a high degree of self-confidence
- Asking for the order more than once

Closings can also be facilitated by the application of specific methods, including:

- The application of a trial close at specific opportune times
- A summary of benefits that demonstrates how they solve problems and meet needs
- The assumptive close when there is a high probability of an affirmative decision
- Special concession close to provide something extra for acting immediately
- Negotiating the single-problem close, when there is resistance on minor issues
- Limited choice provides several options and supplies salespeople with the means to determine the buyer's interest
- Direct appeal quote to ask for the order

Confirming the sale is a critical step to reassure the customer by pointing out that he or she has made the correct decision.

After-Sale Service

Servicing the sale encompasses all activities that enhance customer satisfaction after the purchase. Since customer satisfaction determines the length, width, depth and duration of a customer relationship with salespeople and their companies, servicing is important because it maintains the relationship and leads to repeat business and increased satisfaction.

POINTS TO PONDER — SOMETHING TO THINK ABOUT

1. What is the most effective method that you employ to close sales?
2. What is the most common point of resistance you receive from prospects and customers?

TRAINING ACTIVITY — APPLICATION & ACTION PLAN

Listed below are seven methods to overcome customer resistance:

- Clarifying facts
- Acknowledging partial validity of objections, but offsetting it with superior benefits
- A trial offer to reduce a customers' perceived risks
- The use of superior benefits to outweigh the competitor's offering
- Third-party endorsements
- Restating the benefits and suggesting an obvious choice
- Using a demonstration as tangible supporting proof

1. Analyze each of these methods and identify those that are most effective in overcoming customer resistance.
2. Quantify and qualify each of these methods.
3. Create a listing and index of facts, figures, data and information that can be easily referred to when using each of these methods.

7

Transitioning Into Consultative Selling Techniques

The transition to consultative selling techniques can be smooth or difficult depending on the selling style previously employed by salespeople. Many already employ techniques utilized in this process and will find the transition to be seamless. Other more aggressive and transactional salespeople will find that the transition into consultative selling constitutes a fundamental shift in the way they sell.

IMPLICATIONS — WHAT THIS MEANS TO YOU

Consultative selling employs and blends many existing techniques used by salespeople in various selling processes. The real transition to consultative selling or any other customer-centric method of sales revolves around the fundamental shift in the way salespeople think and their attitude toward their customers. If salespeople find it difficult to make the shift from their own needs to those of their customers, they will also find it difficult to change the way that they sell utilizing consultative selling techniques.

Many salespeople employ transactional sales methods that are perceived as high-pressure or pushy by customers who feel they are being manipulated into a purchase. These salespeople are purely motivated by the commissions they generate, rather than by the needs of their customer.

Transitioning from a transactional sales background into consultative selling will allow these salespeople to enhance their professional reputation and build a stronger base of business that they can rely on over time. While it may appear that the transition will hurt their income capacity initially, they will learn over the long term that they will be financially rewarded for their time and effort.

STRATEGIES, TIPS & TECHNIQUES TO APPLY

Salespeople wishing to transition from transactional or product selling into consultative selling will experience the most dramatic changes in their selling style. While some elements incorporated in consultative selling are used in all forms of sales, there are critical differences that salespeople should recognize when making the transition, including:

Focus

In transitioning into consultative selling techniques, salespeople must make a fundamental change in their sales attitudes. Rather than have a "hit and run" sales philosophy, they must focus on the needs of the customer and craft solutions that uniquely meet those needs with their products and services.

Pace

The transactional salesperson typically will have a fast-paced approach to selling. If they do not see interests or results quickly, they will move on to the next customer or sale. Transitioning into consultative selling requires that the pace be considerably slowed down, where time is utilized to develop sufficient customer information and knowledge regarding customers' needs, problems and concerns. This takes far more time than most transactional salespeople are willing to invest.

Product

When salespeople transition into the consultative selling approach, product recommendations are rarely made up-front to prospects and customers. Salespeople instead probe and question prospects and customers regarding problems, needs, issues and any other factor that might influence their purchase or impact their business. Before product recommendations are made, salespeople must acquire substantial customer information and knowledge and match it with their own expertise and knowledge of their products and company. In this manner, solutions are crafted to meet customer needs, and products are adapted to do the same. Salespeople focus on the benefits that these solutions offer to the customer and the value that is ultimately delivered. The purpose of the sale is not on selling the product, but on ensuring ultimate customer satisfaction.

Account Development

When salespeople transition into consultative selling, they must learn specific techniques to develop information and data, analyze it and develop specific recommendations that meet the customer's needs and address the specific buying influences within their business.

Expertise

Salespeople transitioning into the consultative approach to selling must take time to initially develop specific areas of expertise regarding their customers, products, company, competition and all other key aspects of their business. They must also invest the time to learn specific analytical and evaluative techniques that allow them to blend all of their elements of knowledge and expertise to craft unique solutions for their prospects and customers.

Service

Research has demonstrated that one of the biggest fears that customers have is that salespeople will quickly disappear once the sale has been made. The transactional salesperson tends to reinforce this stereotype. Another fundamental shift in the way sales are made utilizing the consultative selling technique centers around the service levels delivered after the sale. Rather than abandon the customer and move on to the next sale, salespeople transitioning into consultative selling must learn to be highly visible and interactive with their customers after the sale has been made. The focus is to ensure customer satisfaction by meeting expectations and delivering value. This means salespeople must be highly involved in the post-sale process to ensure that service levels are high and value is received.

Customer Relationships

Salespeople transitioning into consultative selling must focus, throughout the entire sales process, on building trust and rapport and sustaining and fostering the customer relationship far after the initial sale has been made. With the shift in focus away from the salesperson and toward the customer, the customer relationship becomes paramount. Every action taken by salespeople is designed to reinforce the customer relationship and to ensure that future sales are sustained and fostered over time.

POINTS TO PONDER – SOMETHING TO THINK ABOUT

1. How difficult do you feel it will be to transition yourself into effective consultative selling techniques?
2. What do you feel is the biggest barrier that you must overcome to make this transition?

TRAINING ACTIVITY – APPLICATION & ACTION PLAN

1. On a sheet of paper, create two columns entitled "Current Sales Method" and "Consultative Sales Method".
2. Down the side of the paper list the following elements:
    - Focus
    - Pace

- Product
- Account Development
- Expertise
- Service
- Customer Relationships

3. List under each heading how your current sales method applies to each of the categories listed.
4. Compare and contrast each to consultative selling techniques.
5. Based upon your analysis, determine which you feel is more effective and productive in the long-term.
6. Develop strategies that allow you to transition from your current method to consultative selling.

8

Consultative Selling Techniques That Successfully Position Salespeople

Too often salespeople will make frequent sales calls to be visible, hoping to get an order by being in the right place at the right time. While this sales method perpetuates itself because it is sometimes effective, it is in fact the primary cause of sales burnout, because it fails to establish career-building sales relationships.

IMPLICATIONS — WHAT THIS MEANS TO YOU

Salespeople are often unproductive because they don't have a targeted list of prospects and a comfortable system to approach them with. They often experience call reluctance that usually rises or falls in intensity depending on their current circumstances and the recent results they have achieved. The major problem many salespeople experience lies not in the economy or the products or services they sell, but is often the result of a lack of self-esteem and effective work organization.

Salespeople ultimately want to do business with highly productive and well-qualified sources of business, and earn the most commission with the least amount of effort. To do this, they need to create a positive environment where prospects are receptive to their approach. In many cases, salespeople's efforts are counterproductive: in their rush to gain sales, they shortcut critical steps in the process and move on to the next customer. If salespeople learn to effectively position themselves prior to their initial contact with their customers, they will find themselves better able to generate new sales and sustain long-term customer relationships.

STRATEGIES, TIPS & TECHNIQUES TO APPLY

Salespeople will find prospects most receptive when time and effort are invested in the development and implementation of a pre-approach marketing campaign. In this manner, salespeople are able to use their experience and expertise to clearly demonstrate their value to prospects before an initial contact is made. Too often salespeople make calls within their territory and then work with whomever will give them an order. This shotgun approach often leads to call resistance and disappointment. It is more effective to work from a pre-selected list of prospects identified by their reputation and need for the salesperson's products and services. This is proven to be the foundation of an effective sales career.

Pre-Approach Marketing Campaign

An effective pre-approach marketing campaign starts with the development of a targeted list of prospects that salespeople can bring the highest value to. Once this list has been developed, high achievers will often ask their current and satisfied customers, including centers of influence, for referrals in these targeted companies.

The key to a pre-approach marketing campaign lies in the salesperson's ability to create a favorable image before calling for an appointment. It should build an image that causes prospects to be willing, if not eager, to talk to salespeople.

An effective pre-approach marketing campaign consists of mailing useful information to prospects approximately every four working days for up to six weeks before calling for an appointment. The systematic delivery of useful business information encourages prospects to perceive the salesperson as a potential business associate and someone who is worth seeing.

Salespeople should refrain from sending prospects sales pieces and promotional items. Rather, the information should be useful and applicable to assist the prospect in their business. Articles from company newsletters or marketing materials are often helpful.

Salespeople should send a minimum of five mailings over a month's period of time followed by a personal pre-approach letter with the salesperson's professional profile attached. These mailings do not necessarily need to be fancy or professionally prepared, but they should be legible, informative and confined to a single page. A business card with a personally written note stating "thought you would find this interesting" should be attached.

With the ready availability of email, such a campaign can be conducted using this medium. However, salespeople should be careful not to create pieces that are perceived as spam and ignored by prospects. Every email should be personally addressed with a clear indication of the nature of the communication noted in the heading.

Telemarketing

Many salespeople resist the concept of telemarketing and feel that it is a demeaning process. However, research has shown that today's prospects are too sophisticated to respond to cold calls. Enhanced building security makes it difficult for salespeople to call without an appointment. Therefore, the use of effective telemarketing techniques is essential to pre-approach marketing.

An effective pre-approach marketing campaign should enable salespeople to convert 40-60% of their contacts into appointments. This compares to a 10% conversion rate for cold calls and only 20% when only a pre-approach marketing letter is used.

POINTS TO PONDER — SOMETHING TO THINK ABOUT

1. Have you ever considered a pre-approach marketing campaign to more effectively develop prospects and new business?
2. If you have used this approach before, what has been your success rate?

TRAINING ACTIVITY — APPLICATION & ACTION PLAN

1. Create a highly selected list of target customers.
2. Identify sources of information such as articles and marketing materials that share best industry practices with your targeted prospects.
3. Summarize this information so that it is no longer than one page.
4. Begin a marketing campaign that mails this information to your targeted list for a minimum of 5 mailings over the next 30 to 45 days.
5. After the mailings and pre-approach marketing campaign has concluded, send a pre-approach letter with your professional profile attached.
6. Contact prospects and request appointments.

About the Author

Timothy F. Bednarz, Ph.D. is CEO of the American Management Development Group, Inc. For over 20 years he has researched, designed and authored hundreds of learning and development programs used by Fortune 1000 companies.

He is also the author of *Great! What Makes Leaders Great. What They Did, How They Did It and What You Can Learn from It* (2011).

Speaking Availability

Timothy F. Bednarz, Ph.D. is available for speaking engagements for your next meeting or association event. He can be contacted at 800-654-4935 or by e-mail at timothy.bednarz@majorium.com.

Bulk Sales

Bulk sales of this book or any other titles available from Majorium Business Press. Inquiries can be directed to sales@majorium.com, or by phone at 800-6654-4935.

Quick Order Form

Fax orders: 715-342-1118. Send this form.

Telephone orders: Call 800-654-4935 toll-free. Have your credit card ready.

Email orders: sales@majorium.com

Postal orders: Majorium Business Press, 2025 Main Street, Stevens Point, WI 54481, USA.

Please send the following books:

____

____

____

____

Please send more FREE information on:

❑Catalog ❑Speaking/Seminars ❑Mailing Lists ❑Consulting

Name: ____________________________________

Address: __________________________________

City: ____________________ State: _____ Zip: ________

Telephone: ________________________________

Email address: _____________________________

Sales tax: Please add 5.5% for products shipped to Wisconsin addresses.

Shipping by air:

United States: $4.00 for first book and $2.00 for each additional product.

International: $9.00 for first book; $5.00 for each additional product (estimate).

Made in United States
Orlando, FL
04 November 2026

90202048R00031